LOVERS ARE SPECIAL™

A TRIBUTE TO THOSE WHO WARM
OUR HEARTS AND FULFILL OUR DREAMS

COMPILED BY
LUCY MEAD

GRAMERCY BOOKS
NEW YORK

This 2000 edition is published by Gramercy Books™, an imprint of Random House Value Publishing, Inc., 280 Park Avenue, New York, N.Y. 10017

Gramercy Books™ and design are trademarks of Random House Value Publishing, Inc.

Random House
New York • Toronto • London • Sydney • Auckland
http://www.randomhouse.com/

Interior Design: Karen Ocker Design, New York

Printed and bound in Singapore

Library of Congress Cataloging-in-Publication Data

Lovers are special / compiled by Lucy Mead.
    p. cm.
  ISBN 0-517-16183-4
  1. Love —Quotations, maxims, etc. 2. Love poetry. 3. Love—Anecdotes. 1. Mead, Lucy.

PN6084.L6 L684 2000
302.3—dc21

                                                 00-024505

  8 7 6 5 4 3 2 1

LOVERS ARE
SPECIAL™

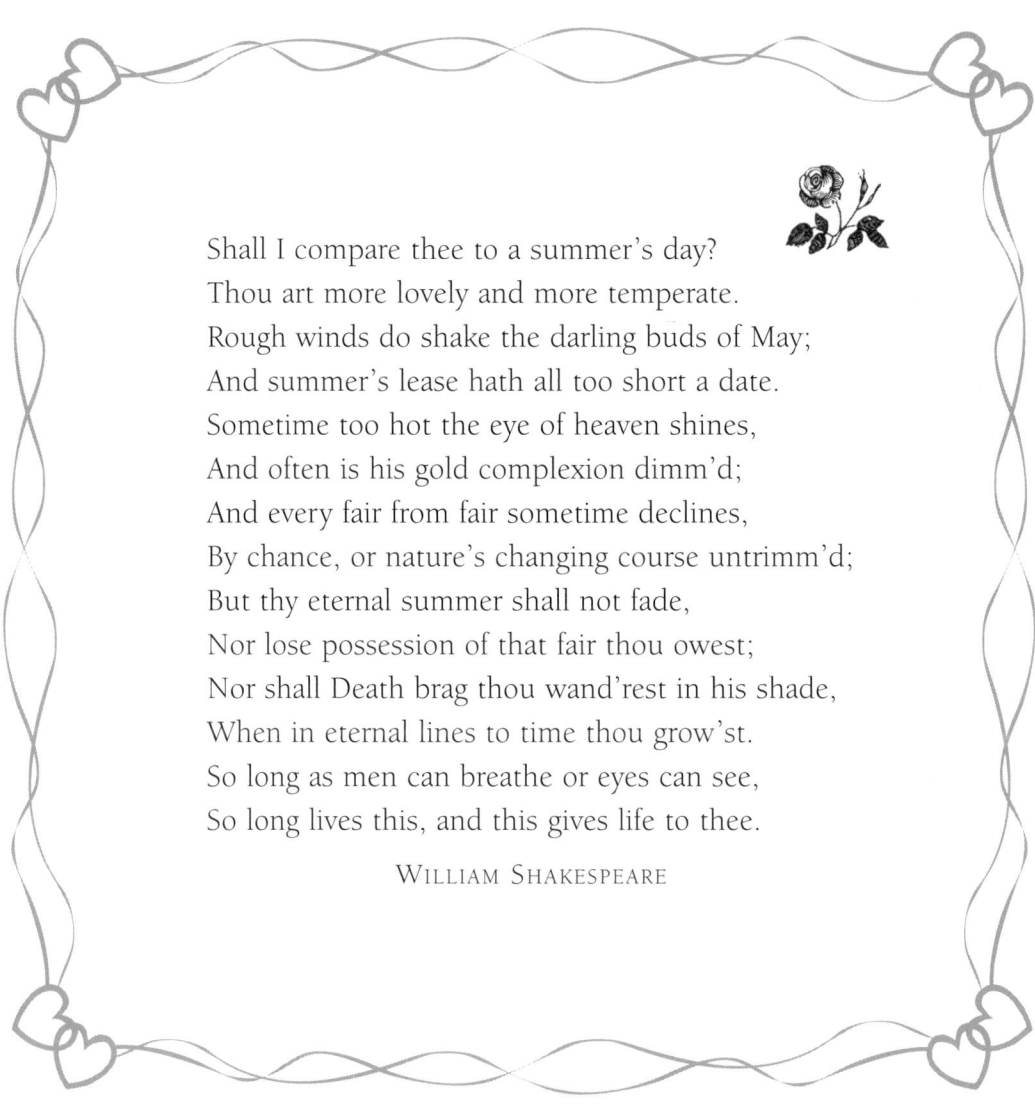

Shall I compare thee to a summer's day?
Thou art more lovely and more temperate.
Rough winds do shake the darling buds of May;
And summer's lease hath all too short a date.
Sometime too hot the eye of heaven shines,
And often is his gold complexion dimm'd;
And every fair from fair sometime declines,
By chance, or nature's changing course untrimm'd;
But thy eternal summer shall not fade,
Nor lose possession of that fair thou owest;
Nor shall Death brag thou wand'rest in his shade,
When in eternal lines to time thou grow'st.
So long as men can breathe or eyes can see,
So long lives this, and this gives life to thee.

WILLIAM SHAKESPEARE

6

I can live without money, but
I cannot live without love.

JUDY GARLAND

It used to be "Love Me Forever" and now it's
"Help Me Make It Through the Night."

ANNE TYLER, *Breathing Lessons*

The word love has by no means the same sense for
both sexes, and this is one cause of the serious
misunderstandings that divide them.

SIMONE DE BEAUVOIR

At the touch of love
everyone becomes a poet.

PLATO

My lover and I don't live together. There's more excitement
in sneaking back into my own house at 4 A.M. under the
eyes of my neighbors than there would be in sharing a
toothbrush.

CAROLE, AGE 49

Money cannot buy
the fuel of love
but is excellent kindling.

W. H. AUDEN

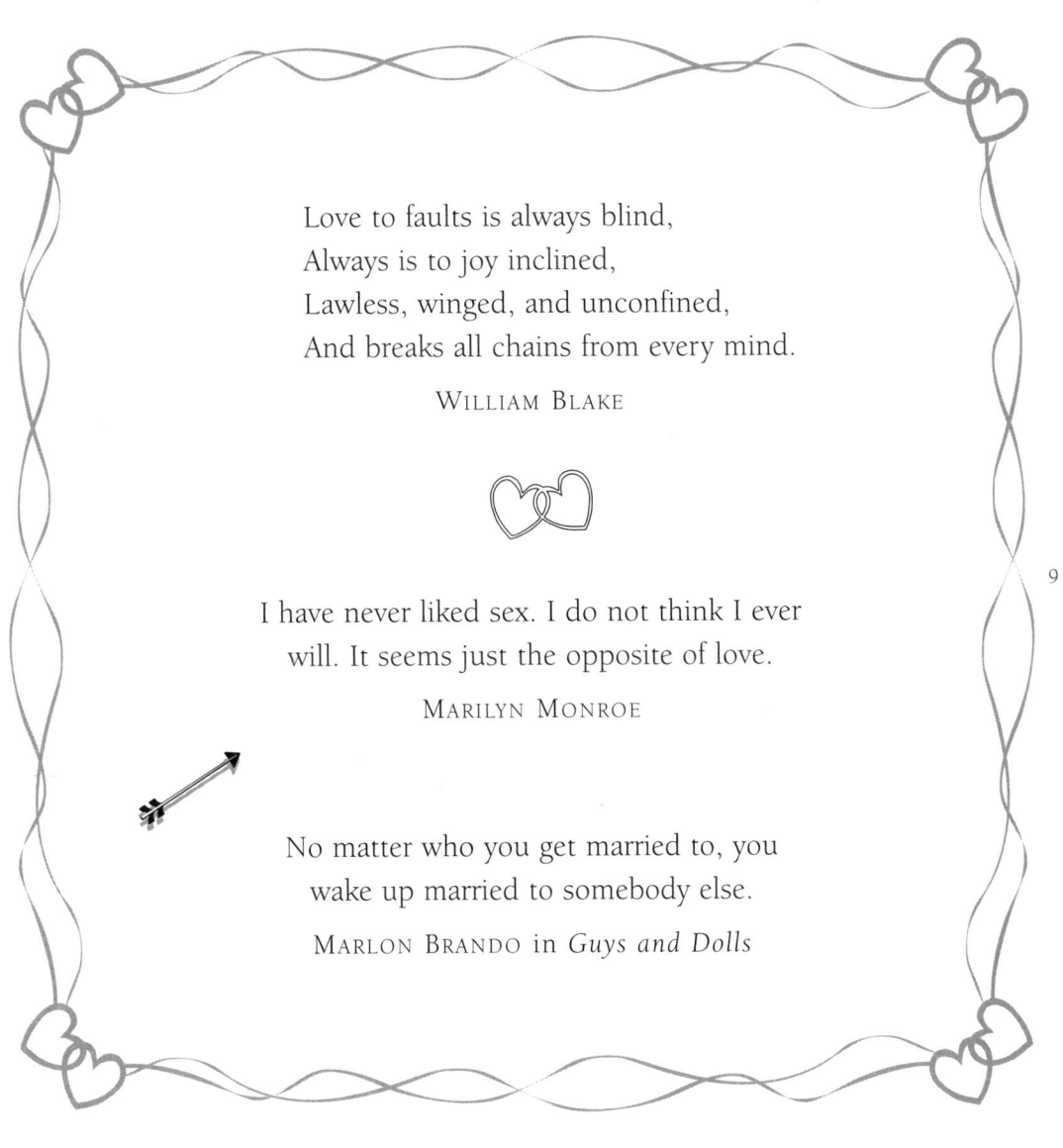

Love to faults is always blind,
Always is to joy inclined,
Lawless, winged, and unconfined,
And breaks all chains from every mind.

WILLIAM BLAKE

I have never liked sex. I do not think I ever
will. It seems just the opposite of love.

MARILYN MONROE

No matter who you get married to, you
wake up married to somebody else.

MARLON BRANDO in *Guys and Dolls*

Love is the triumph of imagination over intelligence.

H.L.MENCKEN

Overheard at Starbucks:

He: You know, I'm finishing law school this year and
I think it's time I settled down and got married.
How would you feel about spending the rest of
your life with me?

She: Frankly, I don't know if I can finish the evening.

By the time you swear you're his,
Shivering and sighing,
And he vows his passion is
Infinite, undying—
One of you is lying.

DOROTHY PARKER

In my sex fantasy, nobody
ever loves me for my mind.

NORA EPHRON

I'm always looking for
meaningful one-night stands.

DUDLEY MOORE

Love is a canvas furnished by
Nature and embroidered by imagination.

VOLTAIRE

Love does not begin the way we seem to think it does.
Love is a battle, love is a war; love is a growing up.

JAMES BALDWIN

Strephon kissed me in the spring,
    Robin in the fall,
But Colin only looked at me
    And never kissed at all.

Strephon's kiss was lost in jest,
    Robin's lost in play,
But the kiss in Colin's eyes
    Haunts me night and day.

SARA TEASDALE

The only time a woman really succeeds in
changing a man is when he is a baby.

NATALIE WOOD

If you are afraid of loneliness, don't marry.

ANTON CHEKHOV

Marriage has no guarantees. If that's what
you're looking for, go live with a car battery.

ERMA BOMBECK

Sex is a bad thing because it rumples the clothes.

JACKIE ONASSIS

Marrying a man is like buying something you've been
admiring for a long time in a shop window. You may love
it when you get it home, but it doesn't always go with
everything else in the house.

JEAN KERR

To attract men, I wear a perfume
called "New Car Interior."

RITA RUDNER

Love is like the wild rose-briar,
Friendship like the holly-tree—
The holly is dark when the rose-briar blooms
But which will bloom most constantly?

EMILY BRONTE

My great hope is to laugh as much as I cry; to get my
work done and try to love somebody and have the
courage to accept the love in return.

MAYA ANGELOU

Let no one who loves be called unhappy.
Even love unreturned has its rainbow.

J. M. BARRIE, Author of *Peter Pan*

I married the first man I ever kissed.
When I tell my children that they just about throw up.

FORMER FIRST LADY BARBARA BUSH

He fell on me like a wave. But like
a wave he washed away, leaving no
sign that he had been there.

LOUISE ERDRICH, Author of *Love Medicine*

SWEETEST FANNY,

You fear, sometimes, I do not love you so much as you wish? My dear Girl I love you ever and ever and without reserve. The more I have known you the more have I lov'd. In every way—even my jealousies have been agonies of Love, in the hottest fit I ever had I would have died for you. I have vex'd you too much. But for Love! Can I help it? You are always new. The last of your kisses was ever the sweetest; the last smile the brightest; the last movement the gracefullest.

JOHN KEATS, 1820

The turtle lives 'twixt plated decks
which practically conceal its sex.
I think it clever of the turtle
in such a fix to be so fertile.

OGDEN NASH

True love is like seeing ghosts: we all talk
about it, but few of us have ever seen one.

LA ROCHEFOUCAULD, *Maxims*

Our new love is surrounded by confidence and commit-
ment. When we face hard times I hope that we can find
each other again in a song we love, a place we enjoy—
even an old joke we both used to laugh at.

MANDY, AGE 25

Men aren't necessities,
they're luxuries.

CHER

I have learned not to worry about love
But to honor its coming
With all my heart.
To examine the dark mysteries
Of the blood
With headless heed and
Swirl,
To know the rush of feelings
Swift and flowing
As water.

ALICE WALKER

18

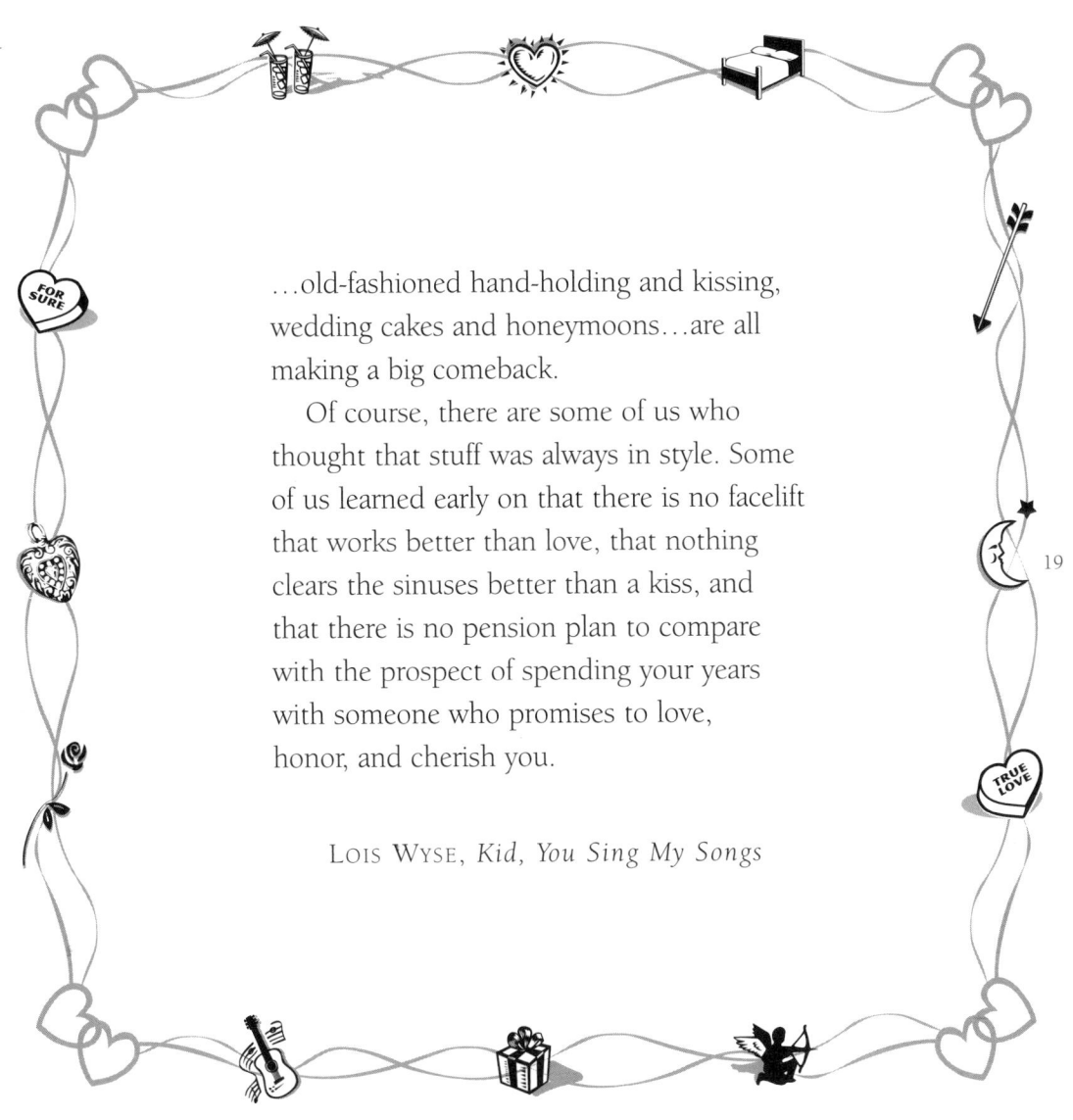

…old-fashioned hand-holding and kissing, wedding cakes and honeymoons…are all making a big comeback.

Of course, there are some of us who thought that stuff was always in style. Some of us learned early on that there is no facelift that works better than love, that nothing clears the sinuses better than a kiss, and that there is no pension plan to compare with the prospect of spending your years with someone who promises to love, honor, and cherish you.

LOIS WYSE, *Kid, You Sing My Songs*

THE BEST IS YET TO BE

Grow old along with me!
The best is yet to be,
The last of life, for which the first was made:
Our times are in his hand…

ROBERT BROWNING

To love oneself is the beginning of a lifelong romance.

OSCAR WILDE

I'd marry again if I found a man who had fifteen million dollars, would sign over half to me, and guarantee that he'd be dead within a year.

BETTE DAVIS

In the eyes of a lover pockmarks are dimples.

JAPANESE PROVERB

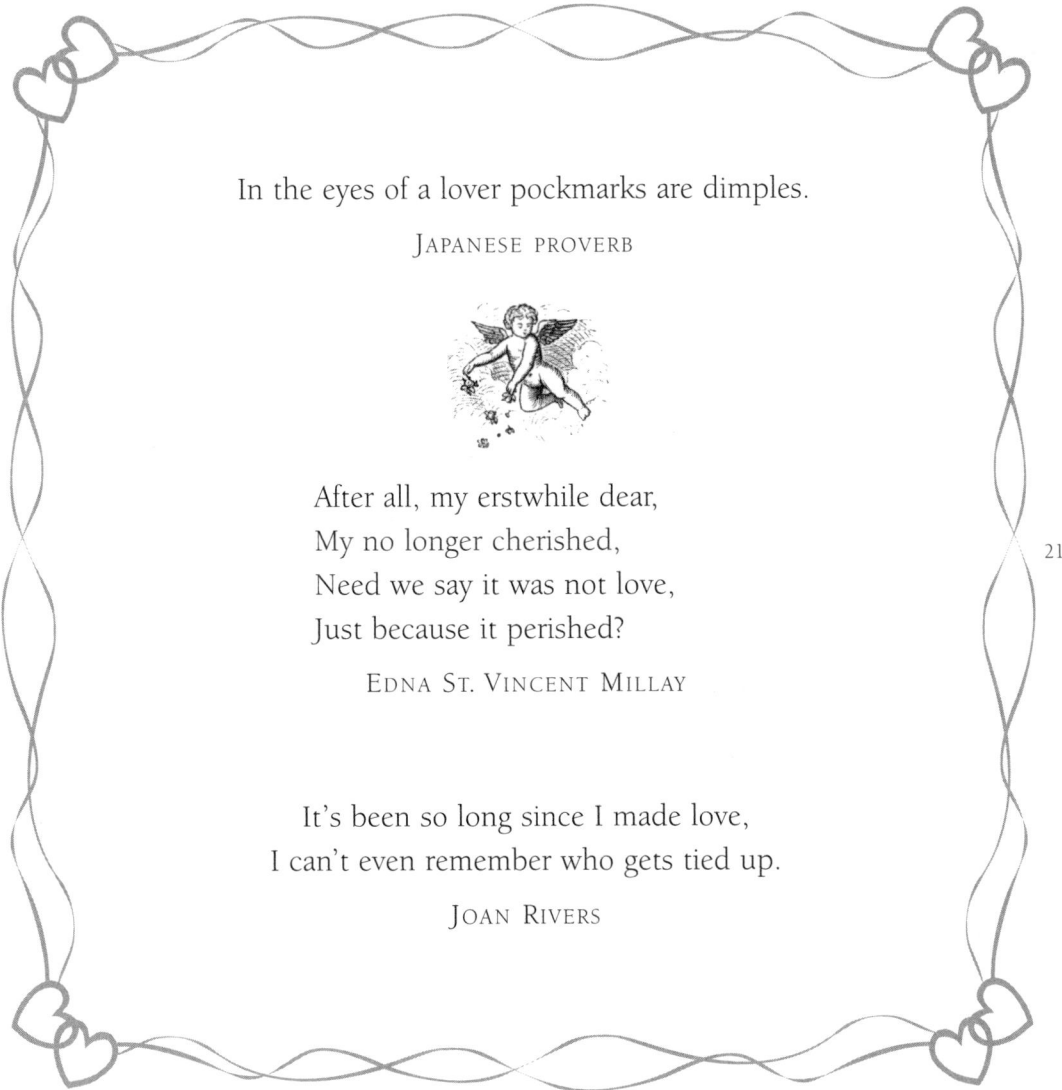

After all, my erstwhile dear,
My no longer cherished,
Need we say it was not love,
Just because it perished?

EDNA ST. VINCENT MILLAY

21

It's been so long since I made love,
I can't even remember who gets tied up.

JOAN RIVERS

Learning music by reading about
it is like making love by mail.

LUCIANO PAVAROTTI

Love doesn't drop on you unexpectedly; you have to
give off signals, sort of like an amateur radio operator.

HELEN GURLEY BROWN

One of the oldest human needs is having someone to
wonder where you are when you don't come home at night.

MARGARET MEAD

The only people who make love all the time are liars.

LOUIS JORDAN in *Gigi*

No matter how love-sick a woman is, she
shouldn't take the first pill that comes along.

DR. JOYCE BROTHERS

Marriage marks the end of many short
follies—being one long stupidity.

FRIEDRICH NIETZSCHE

I think there are two areas where new ideas are terribly
dangerous—economics and sex. By and large, it's all been
tried before, and if it's new, it's probably illegal or unhealthy.

FELIX ROHAYTN, Investment banker

Life is the flower for which love is the honey.

VICTOR HUGO

Sex is one of the nine reasons for reincarnation...
The other eight are unimportant.

HENRY MILLER

Without love our life is a ...ship without
a rudder...like a body without a soul.

SHOLEM ALEICHEM

Love: A temporary insanity curable either by marriage or
by removal of the influences under which he incurred the
disorder. It is sometimes fatal, but more frequently to the
physician than the patient.

AMBROSE BIERCE, *The Devil's Dictionary*

Most women set out to try to change a man, and when
they have changed him they don't like him.

MARLENE DIETRICH

Shopping is better than sex. At least if you're not satisfied,
you can exchange it for something you really like.

ADRIENNE GUSOFF, Comedienne

[Being in love] is something like poetry. Certainly, you can
analyze it and expound its various senses and intentions,
but there is always something left over, mysteriously
hovering between music and meaning.

MURIEL SPARK, "On Love"

A lover without indiscretion is no lover at all.

A lady's imagination is very rapid; it jumps from admiration to love, from love to matrimony in a moment.

JANE AUSTEN

If you want to sacrifice the admiration of many men for the criticism of one, go ahead, get married.

KATHARINE HEPBURN

FRAULEIN FELICE!

Write to me only once a week, so that your letter arrives on Sunday—for I cannot endure your daily letters, I am incapable of enduring them. For instance, I answer one of your letters, then lie in bed in apparent calm, but my heart beats through my entire body and is conscious only of you. I belong to you; there is really no other way of expressing it, and that is not strong enough. But for this very reason I don't want to know what you are wearing; it confuses me so much that I cannot deal with life; and that's why I don't want to know that you are fond of me. If I did, how could I, fool that I am, go on sitting in my office, or here at home, instead of leaping onto a train with my eyes shut and opening them only when I am with you?

FRANZ KAFKA, 1912

I love you almost as much as you do.

WALTER MATTHAU to Jack Lemmon
in *The Odd Couple*

There are never enough "I love you"s.

LENNY BRUCE

Love is…the universal thirst for a communion not
merely of the senses, but of our whole nature.

PERCY BYSSHE SHELLEY

I'm going to the backseat of my car with the woman
I love, and I won't be back for TEN MINUTES.

HOMER SIMPSON in *The Simpsons*

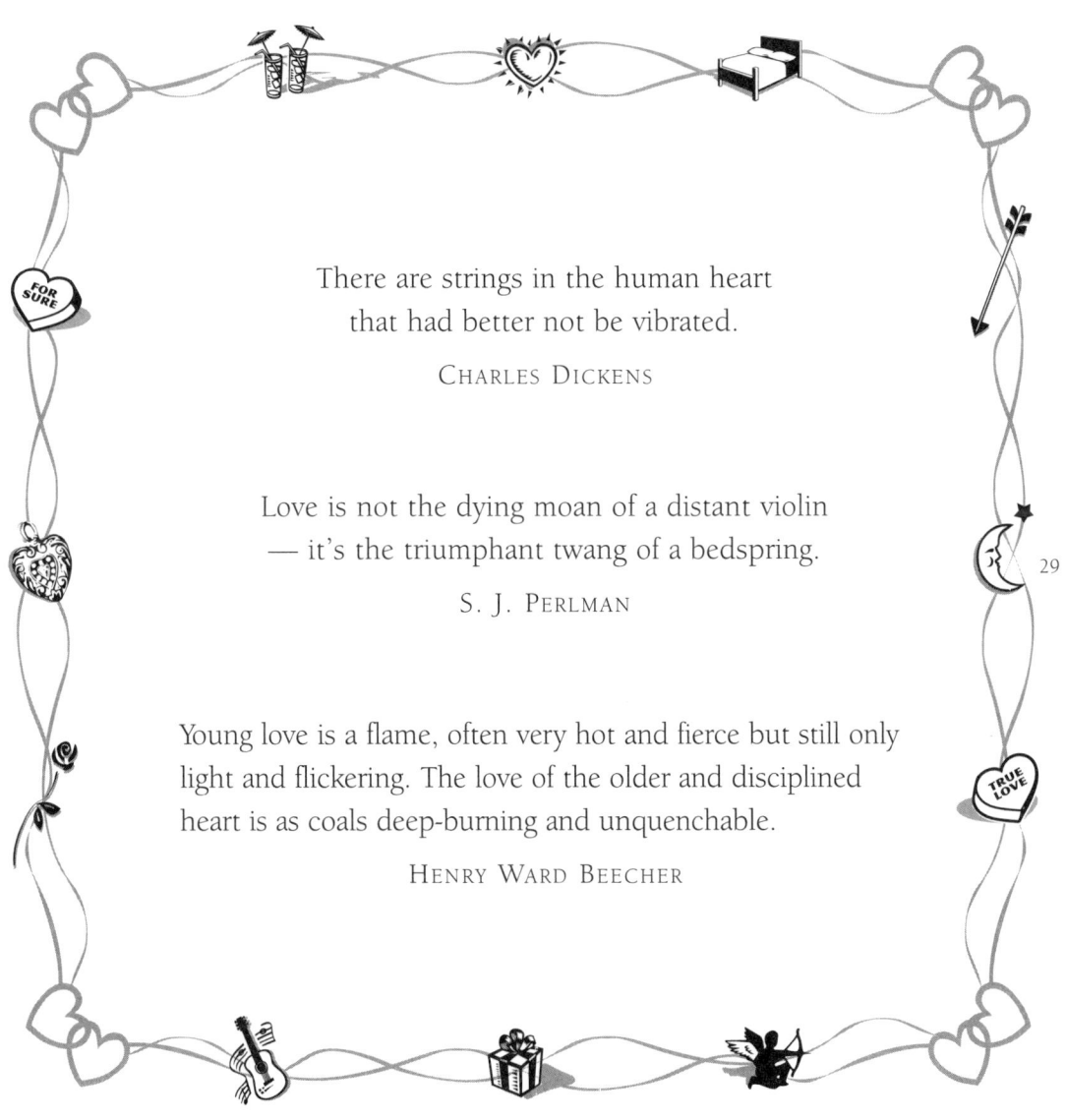

There are strings in the human heart
that had better not be vibrated.

CHARLES DICKENS

Love is not the dying moan of a distant violin
— it's the triumphant twang of a bedspring.

S. J. PERLMAN

Young love is a flame, often very hot and fierce but still only
light and flickering. The love of the older and disciplined
heart is as coals deep-burning and unquenchable.

HENRY WARD BEECHER

29

You mustn't force sex to do the
work of love or love to do the work of sex.

MARY MCCARTHY, *The Group*

★ ✦ ★

There are three possible parts to a date, of which at least
two must be offered: entertainment, food, and affection. It
is customary to begin a series of dates with a great deal of
entertainment, a moderate amount of food, and the merest
suggestion of affection. As the amount of affection increases,
the entertainment can be reduced proportionately. When
the affection IS the entertainment, we no longer call it
dating. Under no circumstances can the food be omitted.

Miss Manners' Guide to Excruciatingly Correct Behaviour

Let us go then, you and I,
When the evening is spread out against the sky
Like a patient etherized upon a table.

T. S. ELIOT

All marriages are happy. It's trying to live
together afterwards that causes all the problems.

SHELLEY WINTERS

Love unbridled is a volcano that burns down and
lays waste all around it; it is an abyss that devours
all—honour, substance and health.

BARON RICHARD VON KRAFFT-EBING, German psychiatrist

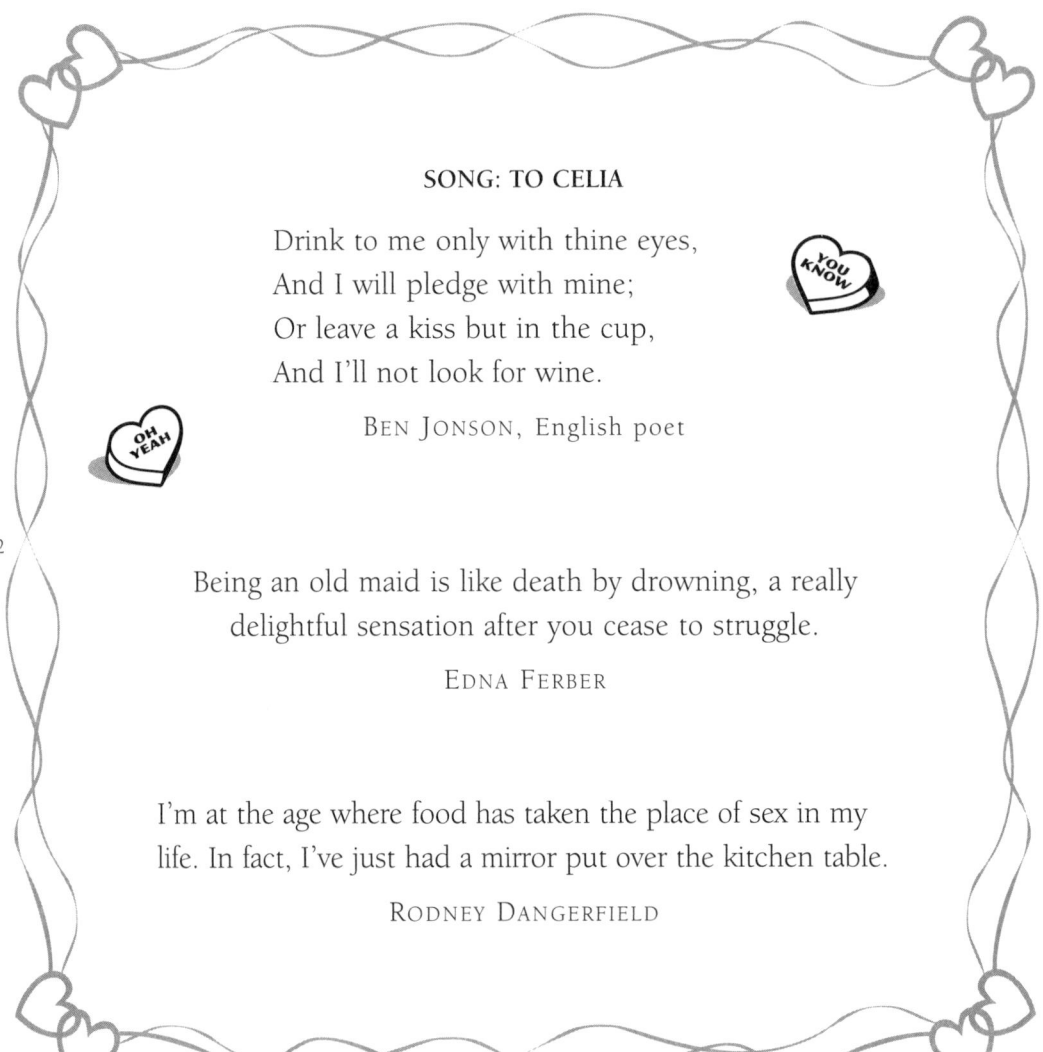

SONG: TO CELIA

Drink to me only with thine eyes,
And I will pledge with mine;
Or leave a kiss but in the cup,
And I'll not look for wine.

BEN JONSON, English poet

32

Being an old maid is like death by drowning, a really
delightful sensation after you cease to struggle.

EDNA FERBER

I'm at the age where food has taken the place of sex in my
life. In fact, I've just had a mirror put over the kitchen table.

RODNEY DANGERFIELD

The last time I was inside a woman
was when I went to the Statue of Liberty.

WOODY ALLEN, *Crimes and Misdemeanors*

...Love is a great beautifier.

LOUISA MAY ALCOTT

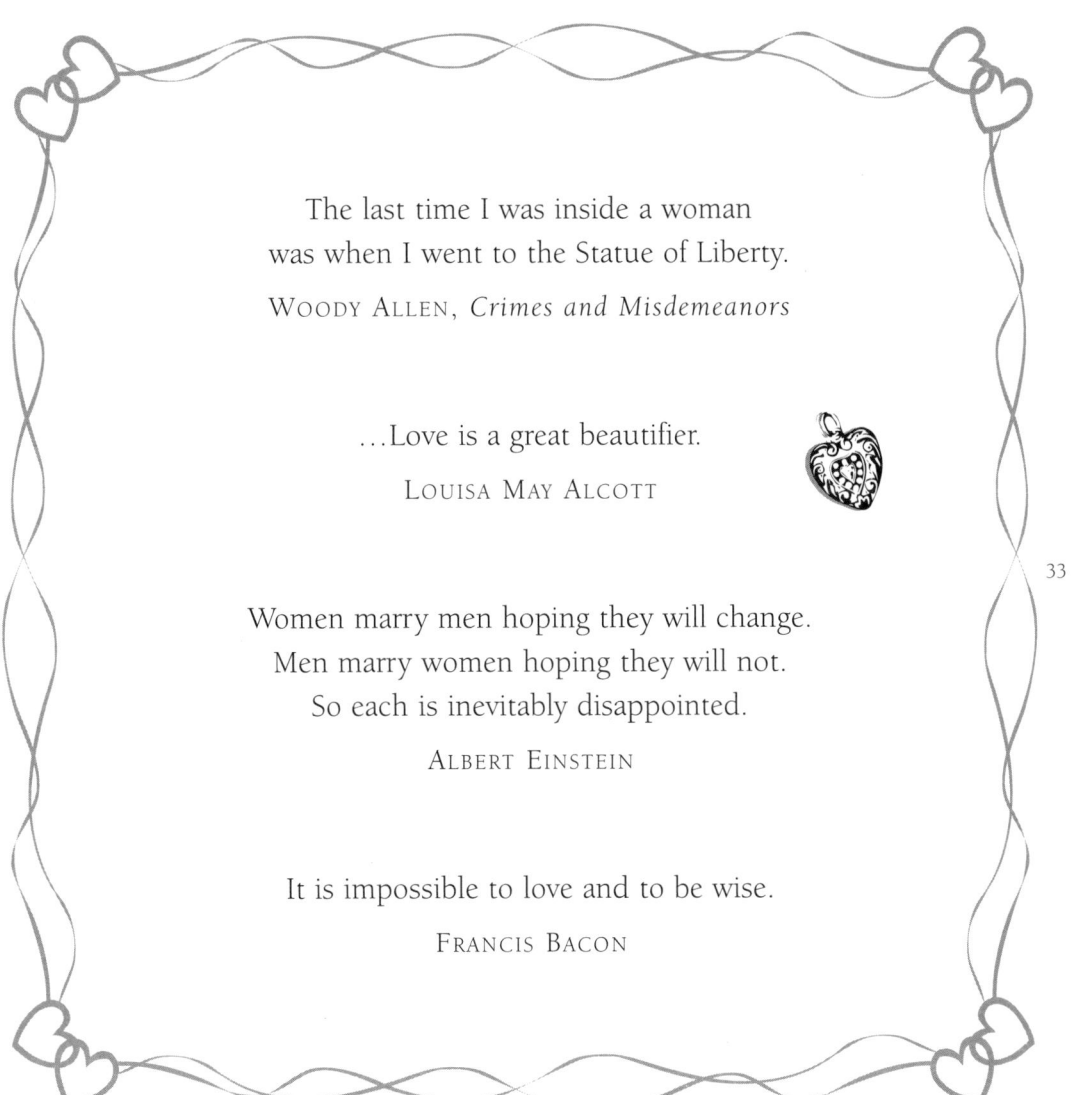

Women marry men hoping they will change.
Men marry women hoping they will not.
So each is inevitably disappointed.

ALBERT EINSTEIN

It is impossible to love and to be wise.

FRANCIS BACON

"Love, shmove," Papa used to say. "I love blintzes; Did I marry one?"

SAM LEVENSON, *In One Era and Out the Other*

Love means making sure you put the seat down afterward.

JOSHUA, AGE 33

See how it works out: it is agreed that we shall be great friends, but if you leave France in a year it would be an altogether too Platonic friendship, that of two creatures who would never see each other again. Wouldn't it be better for you to stay with me? I know that this question angers you, and that you don't want to speak of it again—and then, too, I feel so thoroughly unworthy of you from every point of view.

PIERRE CURIE to Marie Sklodovska (Curie) in 1894

Let there be spaces in your togetherness.

KAHLIL GIBRAN, *The Prophet*

How many husbands have I had?
You mean apart from my own?

ZSA ZSA GABOR

There will be sex after death;
we just won't be able to feel it.

LILY TOMLIN

It is a common enough case,
that of a man being suddenly captivated
by a woman nearly the opposite of his ideal.

GEORGE ELIOT

In my Sunday School class there was a beautiful little girl with golden curls. I was smitten at once…

HARRY S. TRUMAN, about his wife Bess

It is easier to be a lover than a husband for the simple reason that it is more difficult to be witty every day than to say pretty things from time to time.

HONORÉ DE BALZAC

When a woman says that she'd rather sleep with her husband than Warren Beatty, chances are that Warren never asked her.

JUDITH VIORST, *Love & Guilt & The Meaning of Life, Etc.*

Love sets you going like a fat gold watch.

SYLVIA PLATH

Trust your husband, adore your husband,
and get as much as you can in your own name.

JOAN RIVERS

To love a woman who scorns you
is to lick honey from a thorn.

WELSH PROVERB

I've sometimes thought of marrying
and then I've thought again.

NOEL COWARD

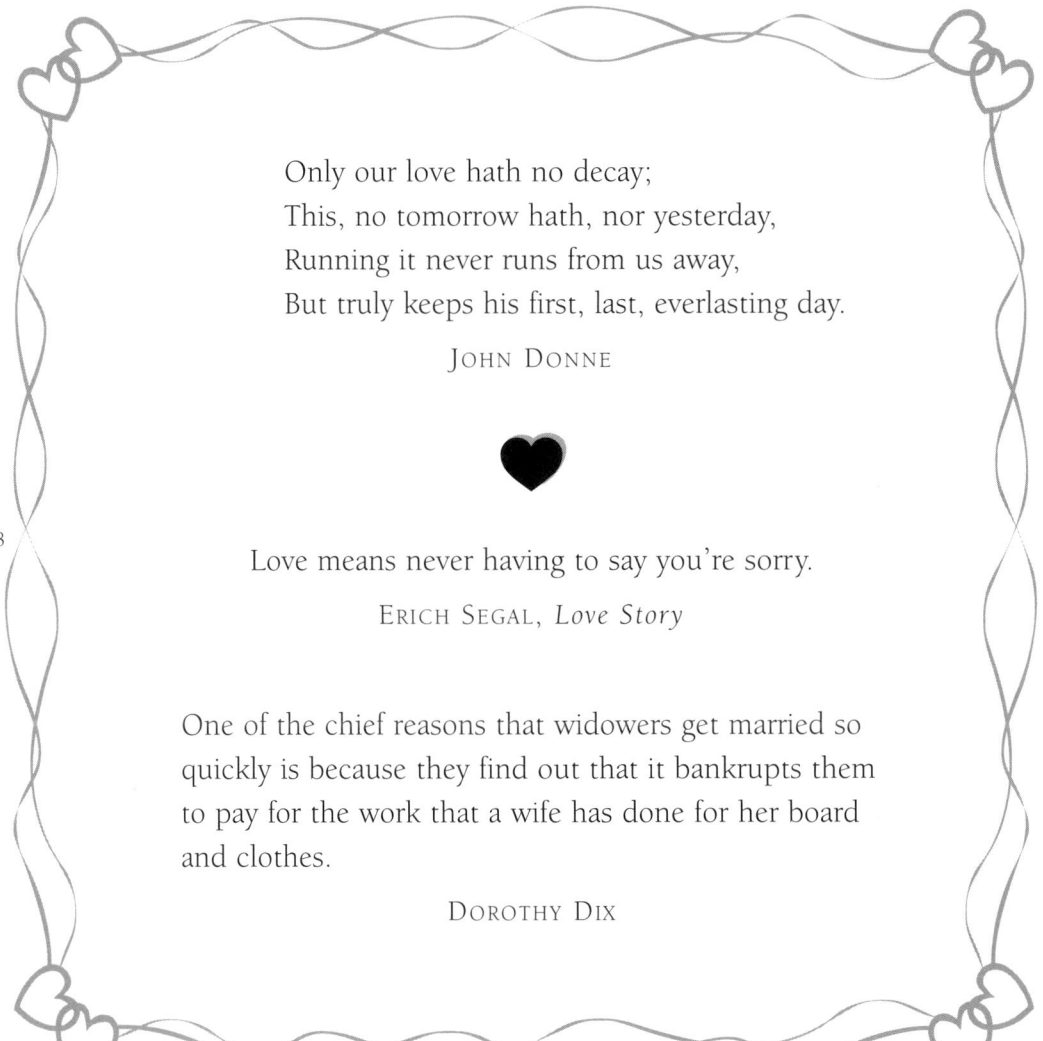

Only our love hath no decay;
This, no tomorrow hath, nor yesterday,
Running it never runs from us away,
But truly keeps his first, last, everlasting day.

JOHN DONNE

Love means never having to say you're sorry.

ERICH SEGAL, *Love Story*

One of the chief reasons that widowers get married so
quickly is because they find out that it bankrupts them
to pay for the work that a wife has done for her board
and clothes.

DOROTHY DIX

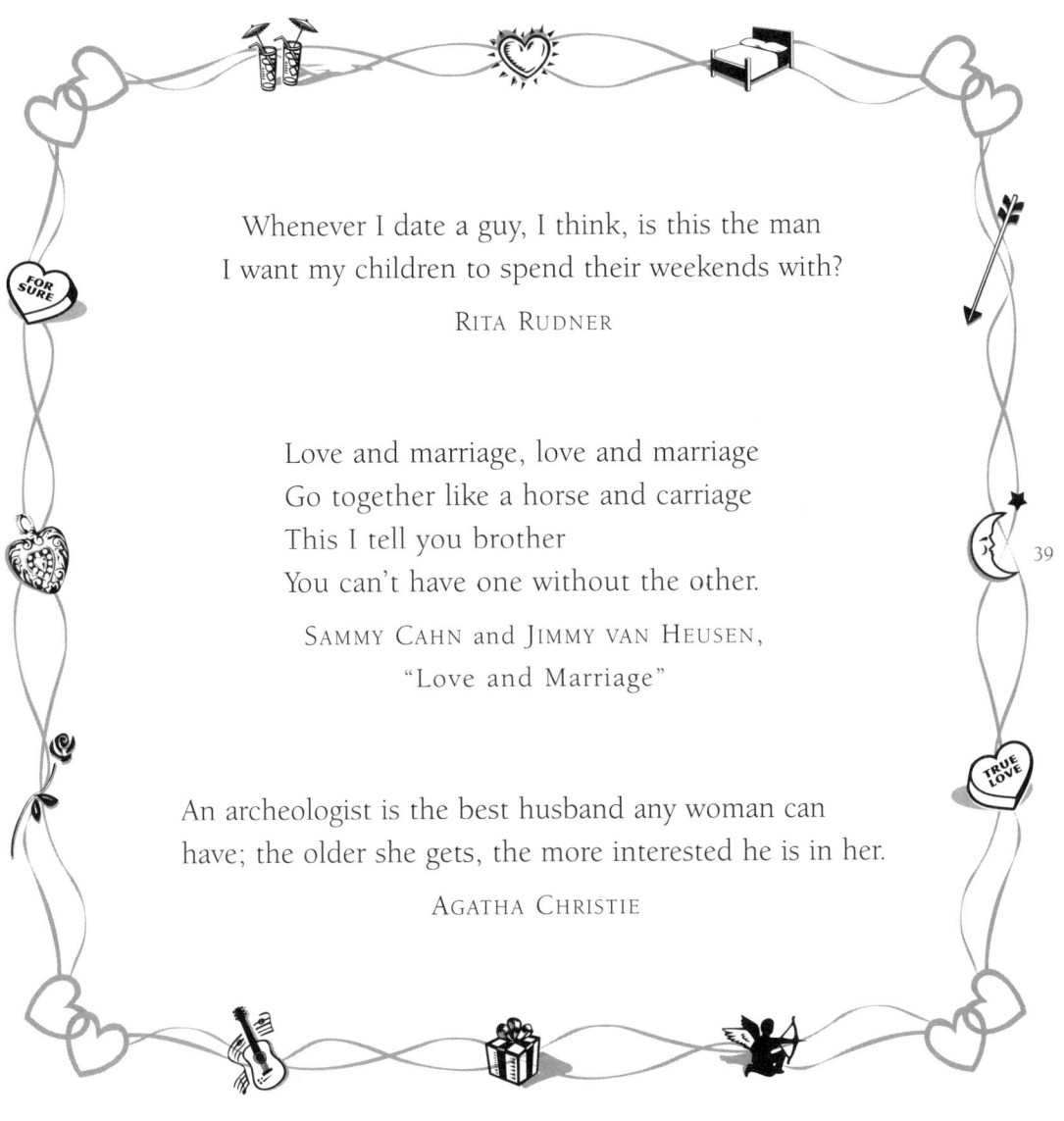

Whenever I date a guy, I think, is this the man
I want my children to spend their weekends with?

RITA RUDNER

Love and marriage, love and marriage
Go together like a horse and carriage
This I tell you brother
You can't have one without the other.

SAMMY CAHN and JIMMY VAN HEUSEN,
"Love and Marriage"

An archeologist is the best husband any woman can
have; the older she gets, the more interested he is in her.

AGATHA CHRISTIE

As I grow older and older,
And totter toward the tomb,
I find that I care less and less
Who goes to bed with whom.

DOROTHY SAYERS

I was married by a judge…
I should have asked for a jury.

GEORGE BURNS

The most important things to do in the
world are to get something to eat, something
to drink and somebody to love you.

BRENDAN BEHAN, Irish playwright

The giving of love is an education in itself.

ELEANOR ROOSEVELT

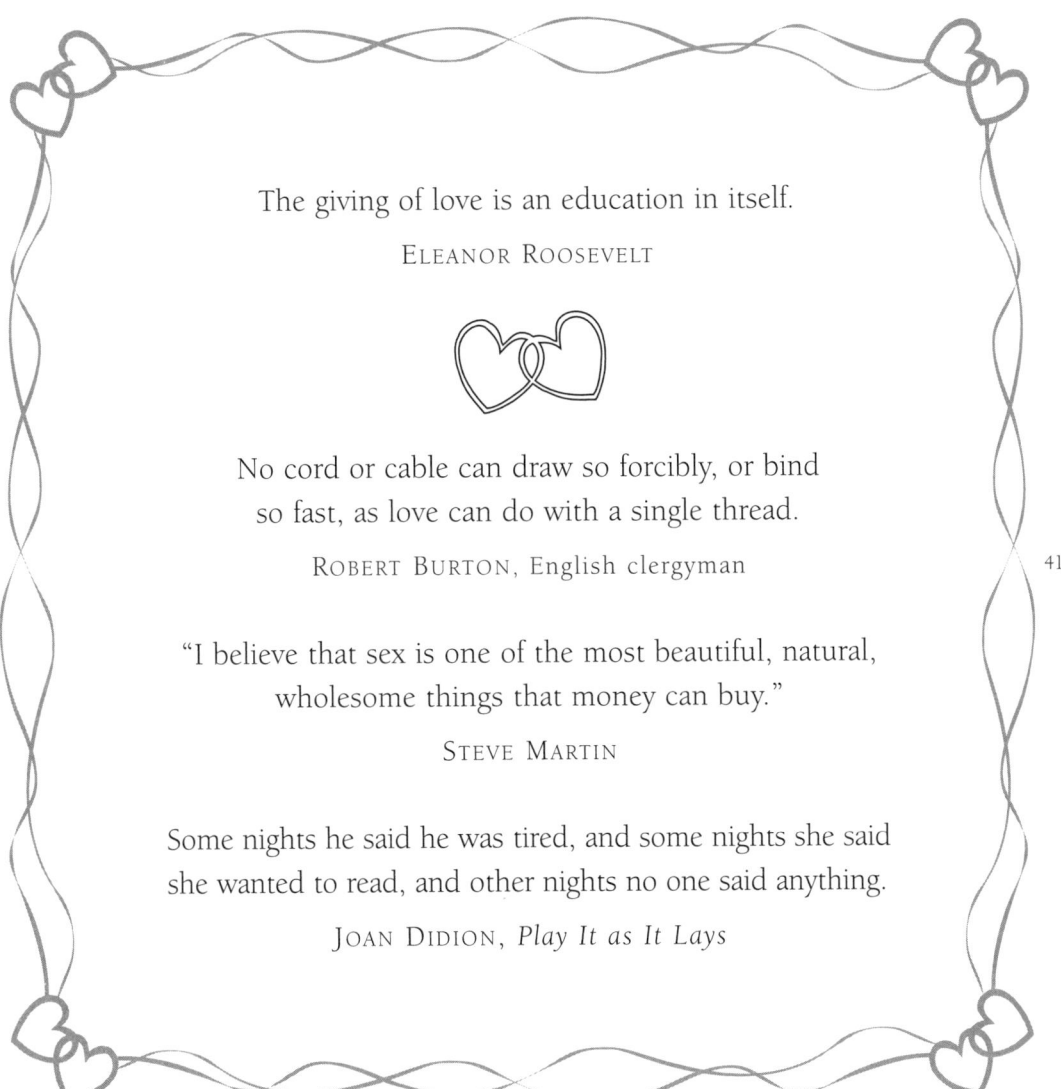

No cord or cable can draw so forcibly, or bind
so fast, as love can do with a single thread.

ROBERT BURTON, English clergyman

"I believe that sex is one of the most beautiful, natural,
wholesome things that money can buy."

STEVE MARTIN

Some nights he said he was tired, and some nights she said
she wanted to read, and other nights no one said anything.

JOAN DIDION, *Play It as It Lays*

Where there is great love,
there are always miracles.

WILLA CATHER

Esther Muir: Hold me closer, closer, closer!
Groucho Marx: If I hold you any closer, I'll be in back of you.

A Day at the Races

Life has taught us that love does not consist
in gazing at each other but in looking outward
together in the same direction.

ANTOINE DE SAINT-EXUPERY

A RED, RED ROSE

O my Luve's like a red, red rose,
   That's newly sprung in June:
O my Luve's like the melodie
   That's sweetly played in tune!

ROBERT BURNS

Love is a fire. But whether it is going to warm your heart
or burn down your house, you can never tell.

JOAN CRAWFORD

Male sexual response is far brisker and more automatic:
it is triggered easily by things, like putting a quarter in a
vending machine.

ALEX COMFORT, *The Joy of Sex*

There is a time for work. And time for
love. That leaves no other time.

COCO CHANEL

A woman unsatisfied must have luxuries. But a woman who
loves a man would sleep on a board.

D. H. LAWRENCE

A career is wonderful, but you
can't curl up with a career on a cold night.

MARILYN MONROE

Romance is the glamour which turns the
dust of everyday life into a golden haze.

ELINOR GLYN, American romance writer

Lie still, lie still, my breaking heart
My silent heart, lie still and break.

CHRISTINA ROSSETTI

The more you love someone the more he wants from you
and the less you have to give since you've already given
him your love.

NIKKI GIOVANNI

Put your hand on a hot stove for a minute and it seems
like an hour, sit next to a pretty woman for an hour and it
seems like a minute. That's relativity.

ALBERT EINSTEIN

Love is the only force capable of
transforming an enemy into a friend.

MARTIN LUTHER KING, JR.

I wake filled with thoughts of you. Your portrait and the
intoxicating evening which we spent yesterday have left
my senses in turmoil. Sweet, incomparable Josephine,
what a strange effect you have on my heart! Are you
angry? Do I see you looking sad? Are you worried?…
My soul aches with sorrow, and there can be no rest
for your lover, but is there still more in store for me
when, yielding to the profound feelings which over-
whelm me, I draw from your lips, from your heart a
love which consumes me with fire?

NAPOLEON BONAPARTE to Josephine

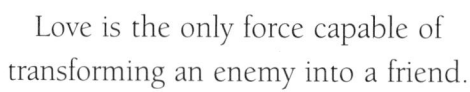

'Tis better to have loved and lost
Than never to have loved at all.

ALFRED LORD TENNYSON

The trouble with some women is they get all excited
about nothing—and then they marry him.

CHER

Personally I know nothing about sex because I have always
been married.

ZSA ZSA GABOR

Sex is like money; only
too much is enough.

JOHN UPDIKE, *Couples*

I've had an exciting time; I married for
love and got a little money along with it.

ROSE FITZGERALD KENNEDY

Falling out of love is very enlightening. For a short
while you see the world with new eyes.

IRIS MURDOCH

I love Mickey Mouse more than
any woman I have ever known.

WALT DISNEY

Just because I loves you—
That's de reason why
Ma soul is full of color
Like da wings of a butterfly.

Just because I loves you
That's de reason why
My heart's a fluttering aspen leaf
When you pass by.

LANGSTON HUGHES, "Reasons Why"

49

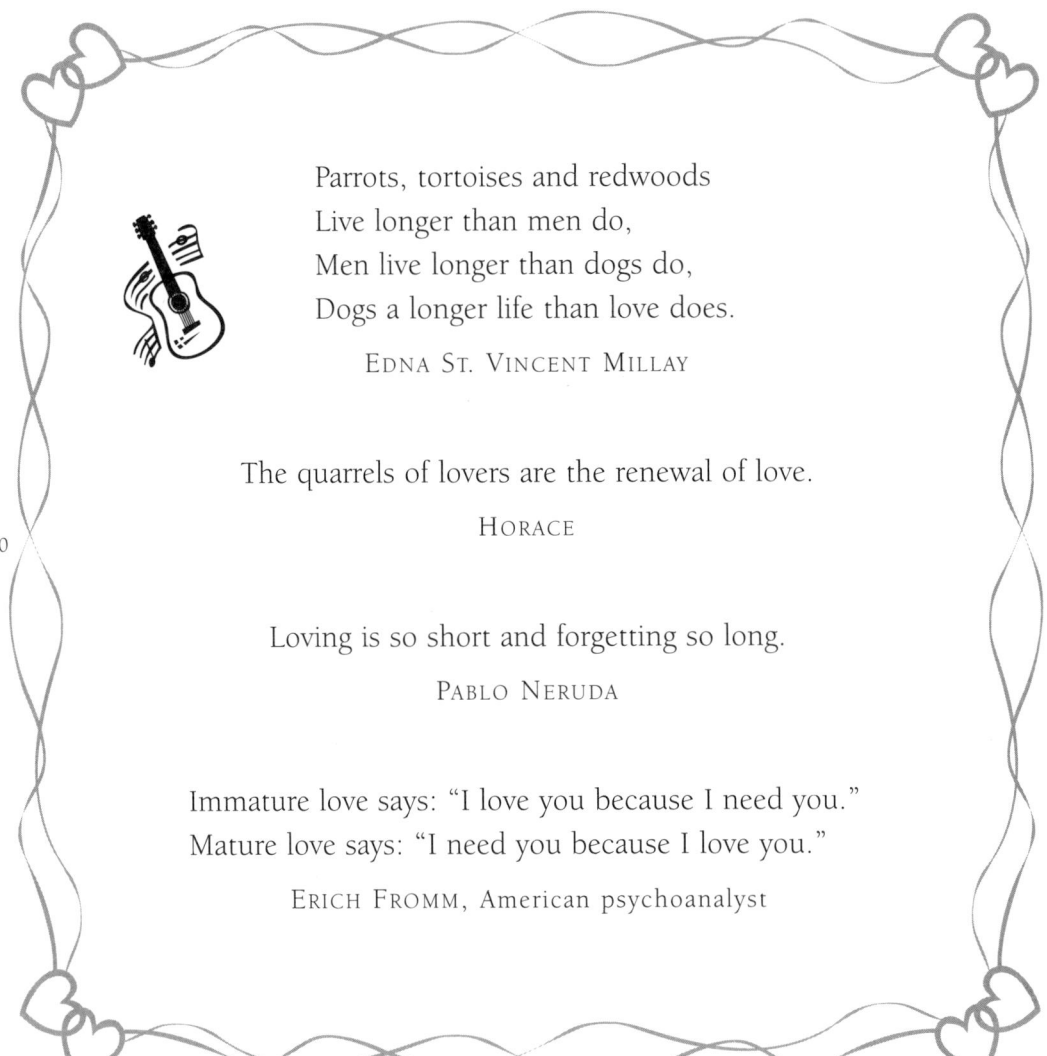

Parrots, tortoises and redwoods
Live longer than men do,
Men live longer than dogs do,
Dogs a longer life than love does.

EDNA ST. VINCENT MILLAY

The quarrels of lovers are the renewal of love.

HORACE

Loving is so short and forgetting so long.

PABLO NERUDA

Immature love says: "I love you because I need you."
Mature love says: "I need you because I love you."

ERICH FROMM, American psychoanalyst

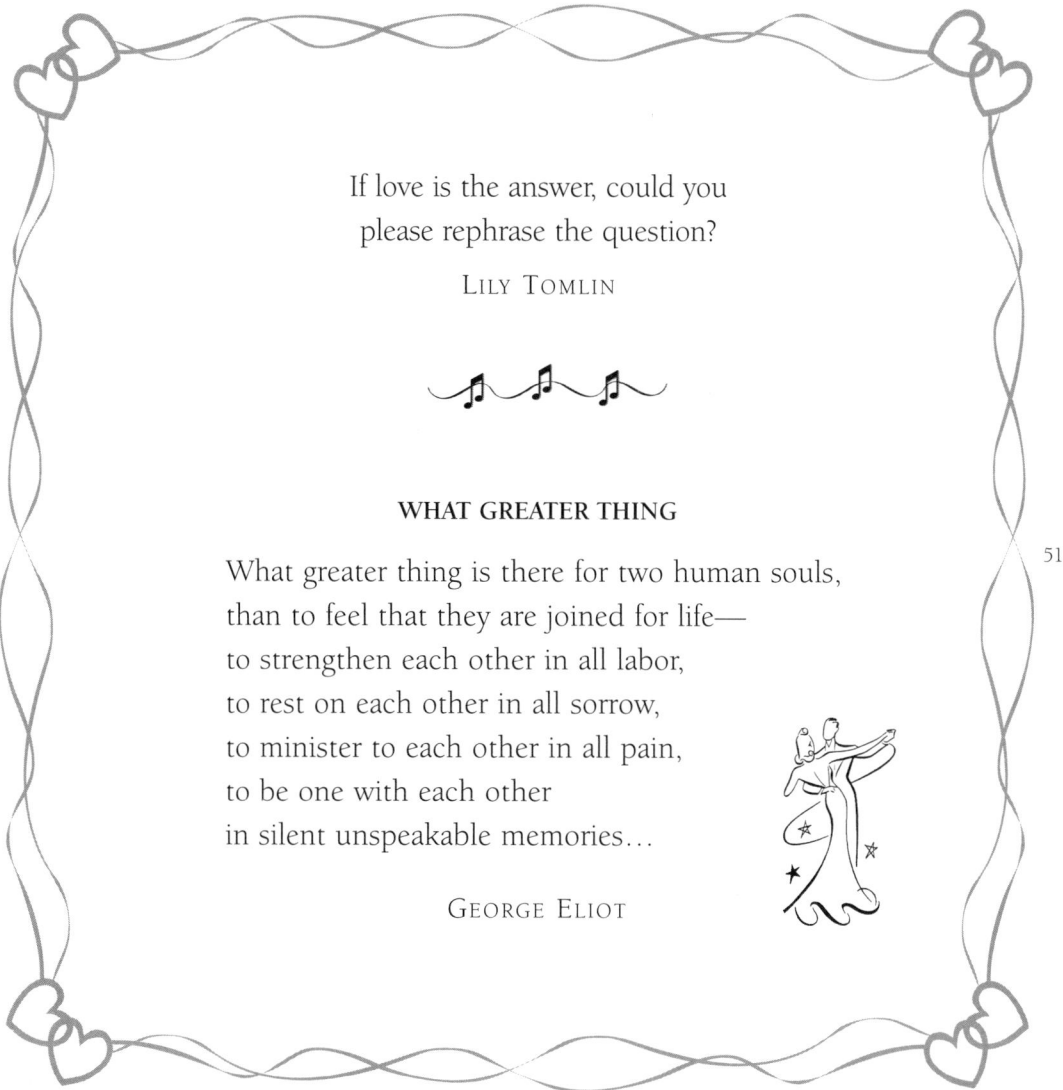

If love is the answer, could you
please rephrase the question?

LILY TOMLIN

WHAT GREATER THING

What greater thing is there for two human souls,
than to feel that they are joined for life—
to strengthen each other in all labor,
to rest on each other in all sorrow,
to minister to each other in all pain,
to be one with each other
in silent unspeakable memories…

GEORGE ELIOT

Love is a kind of warfare.

OVID

To fall in love is to create a
religion that has a fallible god.

JORGE LOIS BORGES

Brevity is the soul of lingerie.

DOROTHY PARKER

If love means never having to say you're sorry, then
marriage means always having to say everything twice.

ESTELLE GETTY, Actress

When love beckons to you follow him,
though his ways are hard and steep.

KAHLIL GIBRAN, *The Prophet*

If sex is such a natural phenomenon, how
come there are so many books on how to do it?

BETTE MIDLER

By all means marry; if you get a good wife, you'll become
happy; if you get a bad one, you'll become a philosopher.

SOCRATES

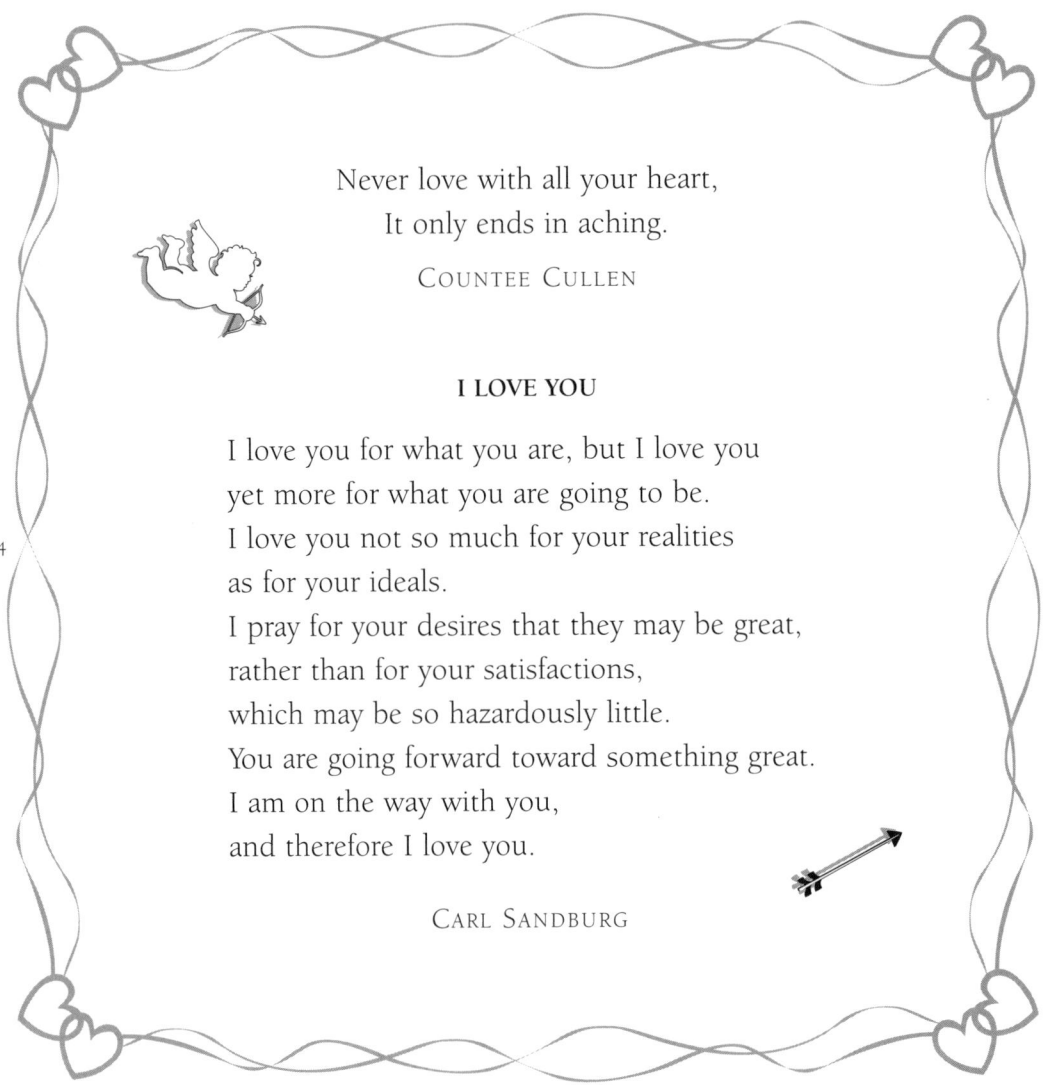

Never love with all your heart,
It only ends in aching.

COUNTEE CULLEN

I LOVE YOU

I love you for what you are, but I love you
yet more for what you are going to be.
I love you not so much for your realities
as for your ideals.
I pray for your desires that they may be great,
rather than for your satisfactions,
which may be so hazardously little.
You are going forward toward something great.
I am on the way with you,
and therefore I love you.

CARL SANDBURG

Think of me as a sex symbol for the
men who don't give a damn.

PHYLLIS DILLER

In her first passion woman loves her lover,
In all the others all she loves is love.

LORD BYRON

Get your tongue out of my mouth, I'm kissing you good-bye.

CYNTHIA HEIMEL

Love is constant, it is we who are fickle. Love does guarantee,
people betray. Love can always be trusted, people cannot.

LEO BUSCAGLIA

If love were what the rose is,
And I were like the leaf,
Our lives would grow together
In sad or singing weather.

ALGERNON CHARLES SWINBURNE

There is no love sincerer
than the love of food.

GEORGE BERNARD SHAW

I'm tired of love, I'm still more tired of rhyme,
but money gives me pleasure all the time.

HILAIRE BELLOC

Sex without love is an empty experience, but, as empty experiences go, it's one of the best.

WOODY ALLEN

Men always want to be a woman's first love…women have a more subtle instinct about things. What [they] like is to be a man's last romance.

OSCAR WILDE

Women complain about sex more often than men. Their gripes fall into two major categories: (1) Not enough (2) Too much.

ANN LANDERS

Grief can take care of itself, but to get the full value
from joy you must have somebody to divide it with.

MARK TWAIN

The chain of wedlock is so heavy
that it takes two to carry it—sometimes three.

ALEXANDRE DUMAS

Southern belles were brought up to believe in "happily
ever after." If charm alone didn't work, they would always
be able to get what they wanted by using their husband's
name. And, of course, there would be a husband. This,
after all, was the South.

MARYLN SCHWARTZ, *New Times in the Old South*

Friendship is Love
without his wings.

LORD BYRON

All discarded lovers should be given a
second chance, but with somebody else.

MAE WEST

This maiden she lived with no other thought
Than to love and be loved by me.

EDGAR ALLEN POE, "Annabel Lee"

Normal love isn't interesting.
I assure you that it's incredibly boring.

ROMAN POLANSKI, Movie director

Was that cannon fire, or is it my heart pounding?

INGRID BERGMAN to Humphrey Bogart in *Casablanca*

Who has not sat before his own heart's curtain?
It lifts; and the scenery is falling apart.

RAINER MARIA RILKE

The only reason I would take up jogging is so
that I could hear heavy breathing again.

ERMA BOMBECK

It is the ordinary women that know something about love.
The gorgeous ones are too busy being gorgeous.

KATHARINE HEPBURN

While forbidden fruit is said to
taste sweeter, it usually spoils faster.

ABIGAIL VAN BUREN

I don't see much of Alfred anymore
since he got so interested in sex.

MRS. ALFRED KINSEY

Love looks not with the eyes, but with the mind.
And therefore is wing'd cupid painted blind.
Nor hath love's mind of any judgement taste.
Wings and no eyes figure unheedy haste.
And therefore is love said to be a child.
Because, in choice, he is so oft beguiled.

SHAKESPEARE, *A Midsummer Night's Dream*

Love is anterior to life,
Posterior to death,
Initial of creation, and
The exponent of breath.

EMILY DICKINSON

I require three things in a man: he must be handsome,
ruthless, and stupid.

DOROTHY PARKER

Love is the self-delusion we manufacture to
justify the trouble we take to have sex.

DAN GREENBERG

Sex appeal is 50 percent what you've got,
and 50 percent what people think you've got.

SOPHIA LOREN

Marriage has many pains,
but celibacy has no pleasures.

SAMUEL JOHNSON

Love is the strangest bird
That ever winged about the world.

LAWRENCE FERLINGHETTI, "Song of
Love and Desire"

Bart, with $10,000, we'd be millionaires!
We could buy all kinds of useful things like...love!

HOMER SIMPSON in *The Simpsons*

How do I love thee? Let me count the ways.
I love thee to the depth and breadth and height
My soul can reach, when feeling out of sight
For the ends of Being and ideal Grace.
I love thee to the level of everyday's
Most quiet need, by sun and candlelight.
I love thee freely, as men strive for Right;
I love thee purely, as they turn from Praise.
I love thee with the passion put to use
In my old griefs, and with my childhood's faith.
I love thee with a love I seemed to lose
With my lost saints,—I love thee with the breath,
Smiles, tears, of all my life!—and, if God choose,
I shall but love thee better after death.

ELIZABETH BARRETT BROWNING

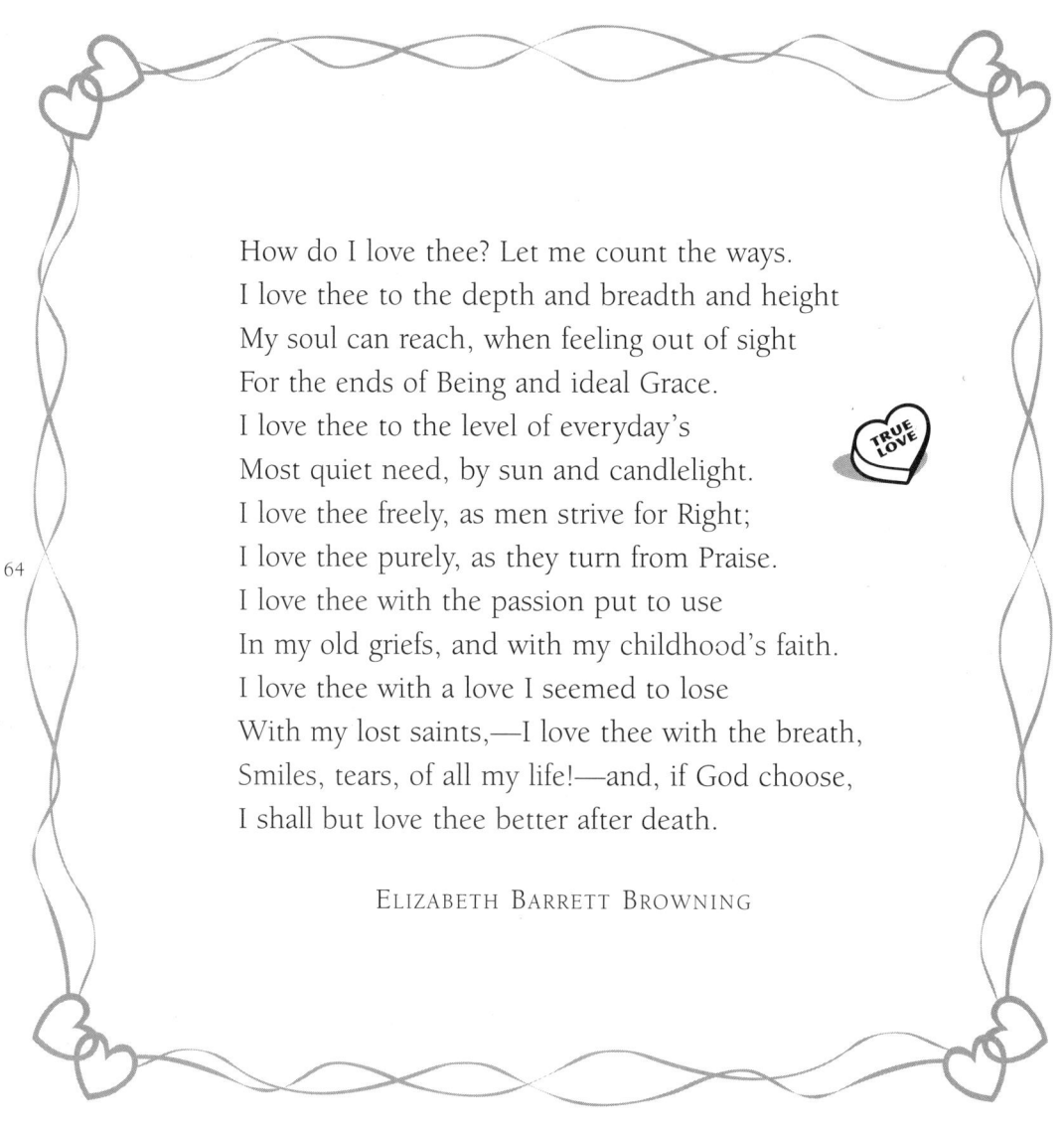